GET TO KNOW
YOUR PET

Guinea Pigs

JINNY JOHNSON

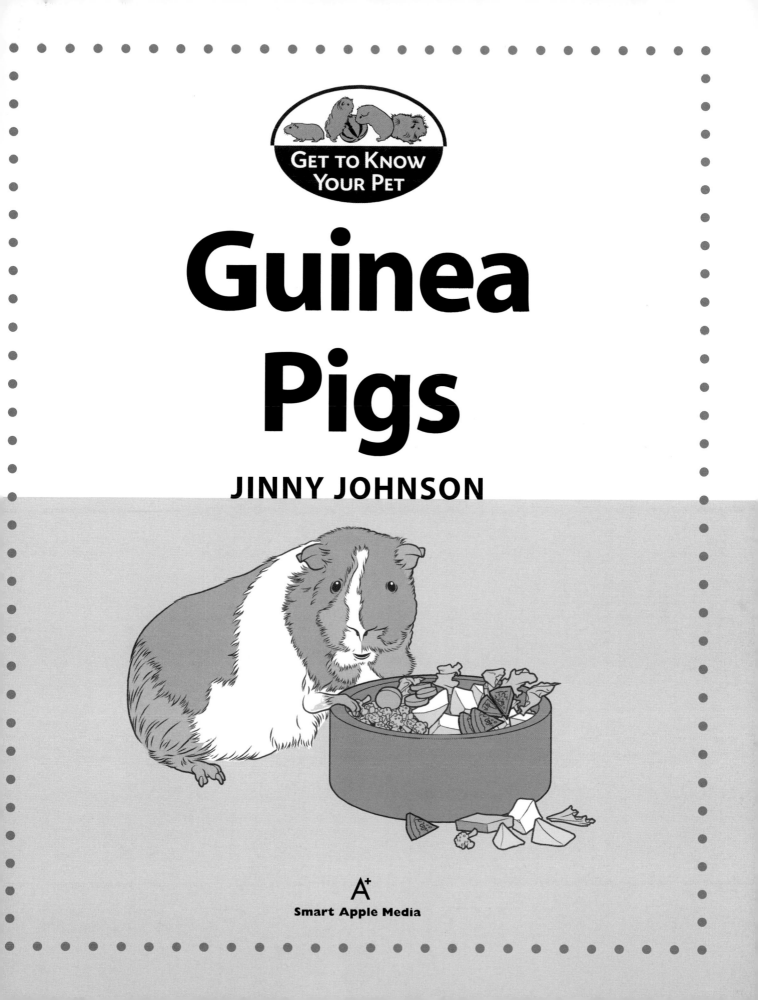

A+
Smart Apple Media

Smart Apple Media is published by Black Rabbit Books
P.O. Box 3263, Mankato, Minnesota 56002

Printed in China

Library of Congress Cataloging-in-Publication Data
Johnson, Jinny.
    Guinea pigs / Jinny Johnson.
    p. cm.—(Smart Apple Media. Get to know your pet)
    Includes index.
    Summary:"Describes the behavior of guinea pigs and how to
choose and care for guinea pigs as pets"—Provided by publisher.
    ISBN 978-1-59920-211-2
    1. Guinea pigs as pets—Juvenile literature. I. Title.
SF459.G9J64 2009
636.935'92—dc22

                                        2007043437

Designed by Guy Callaby
Edited by Mary-Jane Wilkins
Illustrations by Bill Donohoe
Picture research by Su Alexander

Thanks to Richard, James, Ella, Simon and Joe
for their help and advice.

Picture acknowledgements
Page 4 Claus Meyer/Getty Images; 8 PicturePress/Getty Images;
10 Mike Dunning/Getty Images; 12 Frank Lukasseck/Corbis; 15
Paul Bricknell/Getty Images; 17 Juniors Bildarchiv/OSF; 19 Hans
Reinhard/Zefa/Corbis; 22 Jinny Johnson; 25 Jennie Woodcock;
Reflections Photolibrary/Corbis; 26 Peter Cade/Getty Images
Front cover Hans Reinhard/Zefa/Corbis

9 8 7 6 5 4 3 2 1

Contents

Guinea Pigs–Wild and Tame

Guinea pigs look appealing, with their big eyes and rounded bodies, and they can be fun to keep as pets. They are clean, rarely bite, and once they are used to you they can become tame and friendly.

Guinea pigs aren't really pigs at all. They are rodents like rats and mice. Wild guinea pigs live in South America and are known as cavies. They move around in family groups and often shelter in long grass or in burrows underground. Guinea pigs eat only plant foods.

Wild guinea pigs, or cavies, live in rocky areas or grassland in South America. They eat leaves, grass, and seeds.

Unlike many other kinds of rodents, guinea pigs don't have a tail.

Guinea Pig Characteristics

- Small plump body with short neck and short legs.

- Eyes on the sides of the head to see what's coming up behind and beside it.

- Sharp teeth for chewing tough plant food.

- Lives for four to eight years.

- About 8 to 12 inches (20 to 30 cm) long.

GUINEA PIG FACT
A guinea pig has 20 sharp teeth, which keep growing all through its life.

5

PET SUBJECT

Q **Why does my guinea pig try to run away when I go near it?**

A In the wild, guinea pigs are prey animals—they are hunted by predators. So a guinea pig's natural reaction to any sudden sound or movement is to hide or run away. Guinea pigs are always shy animals, but once they get used to their home and their owners, most become less nervous. Be very gentle and patient, and your guinea pig will learn to trust you.

A Guinea Pig's Day

Guinea pigs look busy for much of the day. Their noses are constantly twitching and their jaws are always chewing. They are active both during the day and at night.

It is rare to catch a guinea pig sleeping. They do shut their eyes to take short naps every now and then. They probably sleep for four or five hours every day.

Much of a guinea pig's time is spent eating. In the wild, a guinea pig gets plenty of exercise as it moves around looking for food. But a pet guinea pig needs to run around out of its cage every day. Guinea pigs are clean creatures and spend time grooming and cleaning their fur every day.

Guinea pigs lick their fur to keep themselves clean.

GUINEA PIG FACT
An average guinea pig weighs about 3 pounds (1.3 kg).

Guinea Pig Train

When guinea pigs are out of their cage or hutch, they may stay close together, one behind the other. This is what wild guinea pigs do. A family may make a "train" and run along nose to tail so they all stay together and in touch. Pet pigs may do the same so they feel safe when running around.

PET SUBJECT

Q **Why does my guinea pig sometimes stand very still outside its cage?**

A It may have heard something that scared it. The first thing a guinea pig does when it is frightened is to stand very still and hope that any predator around won't notice it and will go away. You may see your guinea pig do this if there's a sudden loud noise such as a phone or doorbell ringing.

Do Guinea Pigs Talk?

Guinea pigs are chatty little creatures. They make many different sounds, which you will learn to recognize as you get to know your pets.

Once guinea pigs are used to you, they will greet you when you come to feed or play with them. The most common noise you will hear from them is a loud "wheek"—a kind of whistling, oinking noise. Most guineas make these sounds when they know it is feeding time. They soon learn the signs and most "wheek" happily as soon as they hear the fridge door open or the rustle of a paper bag.

Wild guinea pigs live in family groups, so they need to keep in touch through different sounds. These send messages such as, "There's good food here," or "Watch out, danger is near."

Always handle your guinea pig gently and it will soon learn to trust you and be relaxed in your company.

Q Why does my guinea pig bite the bars of its cage?

A Some pigs do this to remind you that it's mealtime and they need something to chew. Others do it because they are bored. Perhaps your guinea pig doesn't spend enough time out of its cage, so make sure it has exercise every day. Provide some chewing bars or sticks for your pet to chew instead of the bars. If you have just one guinea pig it is probably lonely, so think about getting it a friend.

GUINEA CHATTER

● Wheek: a whistling sound used as a general hello or a demand for food. Most guinea pigs make this noise when they see their owner near their cage.

● Purr: a sound made when a guinea pig is happy or enjoying itself, perhaps when being petted or fed.

● Clacking or chattering: sounds made by teeth grinding or clattering together. This is a warning sound, usually made by one pig to another.

● Squeal: a high-pitched sound made when a guinea pig is in pain or scared.

Guinea pigs are surprisingly noisy— especially when they want their supper.

Guinea Pig Senses

Hearing and smell are very important to guinea pigs, but their other senses are also good. Guineas can hear much better than we do and they can smell a favorite food from a distance.

A guinea pig's eyesight is not very good, but it can see nearly all around itself without moving its head. Its sense of touch is also important. A guinea pig's whiskers help it to find its way around and to judge whether it can squeeze inside things. Guinea pigs also seem to have a good sense of taste and may like or dislike particular foods.

Your guinea pig will soon get to know your smell and the sound of your voice.

Saying Hello

When two guinea pigs meet, they sniff each other and may rub noses, even if they already know each other. They may also rub cheeks. This is how each guinea pig leaves its smell on the other animal, which helps them to feel comfortable together.

11

PET SUBJECT

Q **Why does my guinea pig always sniff the air when it first comes out of its cage?**

A It's checking out its surroundings and smelling what and who is around. A wild guinea pig always does this when it comes out of its burrow to make sure it is safe to start feeding. A pet animal probably doesn't need to worry about safety, but this is part of its built-in behavior.

Kinds of Guinea Pig

The most common type of guinea pig has short, glossy fur. This coat may be white, black, brown, or a mixture of colors. Short-haired guinea pigs are probably the easiest to care for.

Long-haired guinea pigs have long, silky coats. They are very pretty animals, but they need regular grooming to keep their coats in good condition. Abyssinian guinea pigs have tufty coats because their hair grows from several different places on their bodies.

Abyssinian guinea pigs have fur that grows in swirls like little rosettes.

GUINEA PIG FACT
Guinea pigs were first kept as pets in Europe more than 400 years ago.

Short-haired guinea pigs are the easiest kind to look after, so they make the best first pets.

Long-haired guinea pigs need brushing and combing regularly to keep their coats from becoming matted.

BOY OR GIRL

It's best to have more than one guinea pig. A guinea pig will be lonely on its own unless you give it lots of attention. Choose animals from the same litter or that already live together. Two females are best, but two males should get along well without fighting. If you want a male and a female, one of them will have to be neutered or you will have lots of baby guinea pigs.

PET SUBJECT

Q **My guinea pig looks sad and just sits doing nothing. Is something wrong?**

A Try offering a favorite food treat. If your guinea pig doesn't grab it as usual, it might be ill. Take your pet to the vet as soon as possible to find out what's wrong.

Choosing Your Guinea Pigs

You can buy guinea pigs from pet stores or from guinea pig breeders. Or you may like to go to a rescue center and give some full-grown guinea pigs a new home.

Wherever you buy your guinea pigs, make sure they are fit and healthy. Baby guinea pigs are ready to leave their mothers at about six weeks. Watch the guinea pigs before you choose. Look for a healthy animal that is active and inquisitive. All small animals are nervous of strangers, so don't worry if the guinea pigs run away. Don't try to grab any of them.

GUINEA PIG FACT
Male guinea pigs are called boars and females are sows. The babies are known as pups.

What To Look For

- A smooth, glossy coat with no bald patches or scabs.

- Bright, clean eyes.

- A clean nose.

- Quiet breathing.

- A plump, rounded body.

- A clean mouth and no drooling.

A healthy pet is a happy pet, so always check carefully when choosing your pet.

A guinea pig litter usually contains two to four young which are born with a full coat of fur and their eyes open.

PET SUBJECT

Q **How do I tell whether a guinea pig is male or female?**

A It's quite difficult. Males and females look much the same generally, although males are usually bigger. You can check by looking between the animal's back legs. The female has a Y-shaped opening. The male does too, but if the opening is pressed very gently the male's penis comes out. Even people working in pet stores sometimes find it hard to tell males from females, so it's best to ask your vet to check for you.

Female

Male

What Your Guinea Pigs Need

Before you bring your guinea pigs home, make sure they have everything they need to be happy and comfortable.

Most important is the cage. An indoor home for guinea pigs usually has a plastic base with a wire top. Never use a cage with a wire base, as the wire would hurt the guinea pigs' feet. The cage should also have a sleeping area where the animals can hide away.

Buy as big a cage as you can. A cage for two guinea pigs should be at least 24 x 48 inches (60 x 120 cm) or larger. Your pets will also need bedding, good heavy food bowls that don't tip over easily, and a water bottle.

Your pets will be happiest in a large cage with plenty of space to move around.

Fresh Water

Your guinea pig must always have fresh water to drink. Water in a bowl is easily spilled or made dirty. The best idea is to buy a water bottle with a drinking tube that you can attach to the side of the cage. Your pet sucks on the tube when it wants a drink. Change the water and rinse out the bottle every day and give the bottle a good scrub every week.

GUINEA PIG FACT
There is a type of guinea pig that has no fur. These are sometimes known as "skinny pigs."

PET SUBJECT

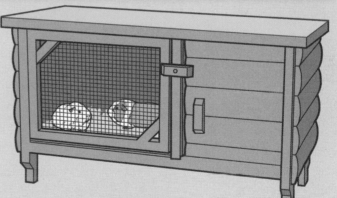

Q Can guinea pigs be kept outside?

A Yes, they can be kept outside in wooden hutches, which must have a living area and a closed sleeping area. Guinea pigs cannot be left outdoors in winter and should be brought indoors in cold weather. A wooden outdoor hutch should be sturdy enough to keep the animals dry and safe from predators such as foxes. It must be raised off the ground on legs or bricks, or it will be damp and cold inside.

Bringing Your Guinea Pigs Home

Make sure everything is ready for your new pets before you bring them home. Check that you have plenty of food and bedding. Make sure that you know how to take care of your pets.

Don't forget—your guinea pigs don't know anything about you and they will be scared at first. Just imagine how you would feel if a big hand came down, lifted you up, and took you to a strange place. So allow your pets to get used to their new home before you try to touch them or hold them. Leave them to sniff around their cage and settle down for the first couple of days, but talk to them so they get to know your voice. Have a few treats ready to encourage them to come to you.

A tasty snack such as a strawberry will help your guinea pig learn that you are a friend.

PET SUBJECT

Q Why does my guinea pig like to eat all the time?

A Because that's what guinea pigs do in the wild. They feed mostly on grass and other green plants and they need to eat a lot of them to get the nourishment their bodies need. A guinea pig is never happier than when it's chewing its way through a big pile of grass or hay. Also, a guinea pig's teeth are growing all the time, so it must eat lots of tough food to stop the teeth from getting too long.

19

Preparing the Cage

Line the cage with a thick layer of newspaper and cover this with wood shavings. These help soak up the guinea pigs' urine. Then add plenty of hay. Your guinea pigs will enjoy snuggling into the hay, as well as eating it. Keep the cage away from drafts and out of direct sunlight.

Feeding Your Guinea Pigs

Feed your guinea pigs dried food, fresh food, and hay every day. You can buy dry food called guinea pig muesli or guinea pig pellets in bags in pet stores.

Make sure you buy food that is made specially for guinea pigs, not for rabbits or other small animals. Guinea pig food contains vitamin C, which the animals need to stay healthy. Guinea pigs, like humans, can't make their own vitamin C. They must eat foods containing the vitamin every day.

Guinea pigs need some fresh vegetables and fruit every day and plenty of fresh hay to chew. It is a good idea to put a hay hopper in the cage so your pet always has clean hay to eat.

GUINEA FACT
The oldest known pet guinea pig was nearly 15 years old when it died.

Make sure you feed your pet lots of different fruit and vegetables.

PET SUBJECT

Q My guinea pig loves to eat dandelions when he's in the yard. Can I pick some to feed to him?

A It's a good idea to feed your pet plants such as grass, clover, dandelions, and shepherd's purse. But be careful when you pick, so you don't give your pet anything that could make it ill. Check that plants have not been sprayed with fertilizers or weedkillers.

Guinea Pig Favorites

Give your guinea pig a good variety of fresh vegetables and fruit. Below are some favorites, but every guinea pig has its own likes and dislikes. And just like us, guinea pigs grow bored if they eat the same things every day. What may be gobbled up one day may be left the next. Always wash food and remove any the guinea pigs have not eaten.

- Celery
- Cucumber
- Cabbage and spring greens
- Cauliflower leaves
- Broccoli
- Lettuce (but not too much or too often)
- Spinach (occasionally)
- Parsley
- Green peppers
- Carrots
- Peas in their pods
- Slices of tomato
- Slices of orange, apple, or melon (remove pips or seeds)
- Carrots, cut into pieces
- Strawberries
- Grapes

Exercising Your Guinea Pigs

If you have a yard, your guinea pigs will enjoy running outdoors. The safest way to let them run around is to buy or make a grazing run.

A grazing run is made of wood and mesh with a door or flap at each end. It needs a covered section to give the guinea pigs some shade.

When your guinea pigs are in their run, make sure the grass has not been sprayed with chemicals. Never put them on wet grass and move the run regularly so they always have something fresh to nibble. Give them water and don't leave them out in hot weather.

22

GUINEA PIG FACT
Guinea pigs are kept as food animals in South American countries such as Peru.

Guinea pigs like to have some time outdoors nibbling on fresh grass, but make sure they are safe.

Indoor Exercise

In winter, or if you don't have a yard, your pets will enjoy time out of their cage indoors. Make them a large shallow play box where they can run around, or let them out in a safe room. Check that there are no wires they can chew or tight spots where they could become trapped. Give them cardboard tubes or boxes to run in and out of.

Let your guinea pigs exercise in an indoor play area in wet or cold weather.

PET SUBJECT

Q **I've seen my guinea pig eating its poop. Is this normal?**

A Yes, it is, and it's important for guinea pigs to do this. Much of their food is hard for their bodies to digest and use. When a guinea pig eats its droppings, the food passes through its body a second time, so the animals can take more nourishment from it. Guinea pigs don't eat all their droppings— just the soft kind, which they take straight from their bottoms.

Holding and Handling

Be very gentle and careful when you pick up or hold your guinea pig. They are easily frightened. A scared guinea pig can never be a loving pet.

Always hold your guinea pig with both hands. Support its weight with one hand and hold it across the shoulders with the other hand. Talk to it quietly as you lift it up to help it not feel frightened. It's safest for young children to sit down and stroke the guinea pig gently on their lap.

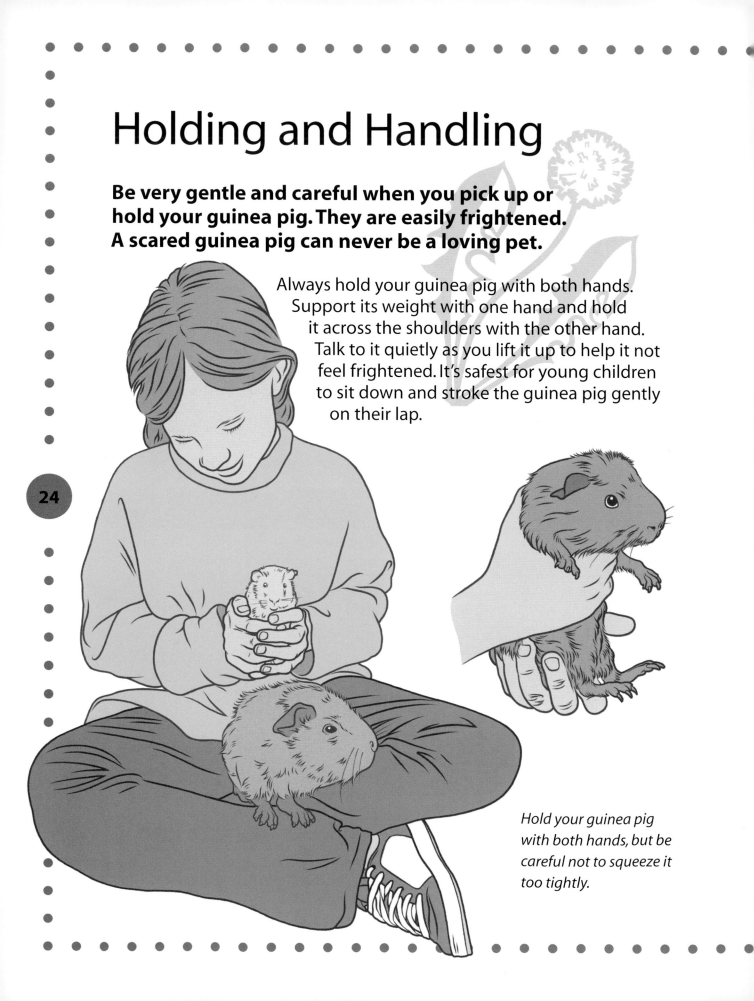

Hold your guinea pig with both hands, but be careful not to squeeze it too tightly.

Tail or No Tail?

A guinea pig does have a tiny tail, but you can't really see it. Lots of animals have long tails to help them balance as they jump or climb. Guinea pigs don't climb, so they don't need a long tail.

PET SUBJECT

Q **Why does my guinea pig struggle when I reach into its cage?**

A Imagine how you would feel if something large came down from above and grabbed you. That's how it feels for your guinea pig. Try to sit down at your guinea pig's level, instead of pouncing from a great height. Lift your pet carefully and put it on your lap as you sit on the floor. Stroke it gently and try rubbing under its chin—lots of guinea pigs love this. You could offer your pet a favorite snack while it is on your lap.

Grooming and Care

Short-haired guinea pigs don't really need grooming, but a gentle brush or comb keeps their coats clean and helps you get to know them.

Brushing also helps your guinea pigs get used to being handled by you. Many guinea pigs enjoy being brushed.

A long-haired guinea pig needs regular brushing and combing. Gently untangle any knots in the fur and take out any bits of dirt or hay. Then carefully comb through your pet's coat. As you groom your guinea pig, look for sores or scratches. Check your guinea pig's claws, too. If they are very long, you might need to ask your vet to trim them.

Brushing and combing helps remove any loose fur from your guinea pig.

Cleaning the Cage

Every day, remove dirty or wet hay and any droppings and give the guinea pigs some fresh hay. Take out any fresh food they haven't eaten.

At least once a week, take everything out of the cage, wash the base of the cage well, and dry it thoroughly. Line it with fresh newspaper, clean woodshavings, and hay.

PET SUBJECT

Q Why does my guinea pig rub its bottom on the cage floor when I've just cleaned it out?

A Your pet is putting its own smell back by rubbing itself against the floor. It's nice to have a clean cage, but a pig likes its home to smell of itself. This is like marking its territory in the wild and makes it feel safe and happy.

For Parents and Caregivers

Caring for any pet is a big responsibility. Looking after an animal takes time and money, and children cannot do everything themselves. You'll need to show your child how to behave around the animal, provide what the pet needs, and make sure it is healthy and has any necessary care from the vet.

A guinea pig may live for seven or eight years, so you're taking on a long commitment. That said, helping care for a pet and learning to respect it and handle it gently are very good for children and can be great fun too.

CHOOSING GUINEA PIGS

Be careful to choose healthy animals. If you buy guinea pigs from a pet store, take them to the vet as soon as possible for a health check. Ask the vet to check the sex of the animals, too. Pet stores may get this wrong!

If you find your pets at a rescue center, be prepared for lots of questions about your life and your home. Don't be offended—they are trying to do the best for their animals and to make

sure that you have pets that suit you. Short-haired guinea pigs are the best choice for children because they are the easiest to look after. When you've chosen your pets, you'll need a carrying cage or a sturdy cardboard box to bring them home in. A cat carrier is fine, or you could ask your vet for a carrying box.

HOUSING

You'll need to organize a hutch or cage and run for your guinea pigs, which can be quite expensive. You'll also need to help your child clean out the animals' home regularly.

FEEDING

Once your guinea pigs are settled, a child can bring them dry food and change their water daily. Children can give the animals fresh food too, but make sure they know what is safe for the animals to eat.

Like us, guinea pigs cannot store vitamin C, so they need some every day. Make sure your pets have dried food that contains the vitamin as well as vitamin-C rich fruit and vegetables.

HANDLING

It's important to show your child how to handle guinea pigs properly and teach them that they are not cuddly toys. If a child handles a guinea pig roughly, it will be nervous and insecure, so it will unlikely ever be a loving pet. Teach your child to respect animals and to always treat them gently. Don't let your child grab a guinea pig and speak loudly, especially at first when the animals will be anxious.

HEALTH CHECK

Keep an eye on your guinea pigs' health and watch for signs of illness. Check regularly for signs of parasites and claws growing too long. Take your pets to the vet if their claws need clipping. Keep an eye open for any skin problems or itches.

Check your guinea pig's teeth too—if they look very long, your pet needs more things to chew.

Weighing your guinea pig regularly is a good way to check that it is fit and well and not getting too fat. Weight loss can be a sign of illness.

Glossary

breeder
Someone who keeps guinea pigs and sells the young they produce.

burrow
A hole dug in the ground where a wild guinea pig makes its home and cares for its young.

droppings
A guinea pig's poop.

fertilizer
Chemicals put on grass and other plants to help them grow.

grooming
Caring for and cleaning the fur. You can groom your guinea pig by brushing or combing its fur.

hay hopper
A wire rack that fits on the side of a cage. Supplies of hay can be put into the hopper to keep the hay clean and dry.

litter
A group of young from the same mother.

neutering
An operation performed by a vet on an animal so that it cannot have babies.

nourishment
The vitamins, minerals, and proteins that animals need from food in order to live and grow.

parasites
Tiny creatures such as fleas, lice, and mites, which can live on a guinea pig's body.

predator
An animal that kills and eats other animals.

prey
Animals that are hunted and eaten by other animals.

rodent
A group of mammals that includes rats and mice as well as guinea pigs.

territory
An animal's home area where it spends most of its time.

vitamin C
A substance contained in food that is necessary for good health; vitamin C can help prevent some illnesses.

weedkiller
Chemicals used to kill weeds in the yard, which can be poisonous to pets.

Web Sites

For Kids:

ASPCA Animaland: Pet Care

http://www.aspca.org/site/PageServer?pagename=kids_pc_home
The American Society for the Prevention of Cruelty to Animals has some excellent advice about caring for your pets.

Guinea Lynx: Guinea Pig Care Guide

http://www.guinealynx.com/healthycavy.html
A comprehensive site with lots of medical advice put together by guinea pig owners.

Healthy Pet.com: Guinea Pig Care

http://www.healthypet.com/library_view.aspx?ID=67
The American Animal Hospital Association offers advice on caring for guinea pigs.

Rabbit, Horse, and Other Pet Care

http://www.hsus.org/pets/pet_care/rabbit_horse_and_other_pet_care/
The Humane Society of the United States offers pet care essentials for many types of pets, including guinea pigs.

For Teachers:

Best Friends Animal Society: Humane Education Classroom Resources

http://www.bestfriends.org/atthesanctuary/humaneeducation/
classroomresources.cfm
Lesson plans and lots of information about treating animals humanely.

Education World Lesson Plans: Pet Week Lessons for Every Grade

http://www.educationworld.com/a_lesson/lesson/lesson311.shtml
Use the topic of pets to engage your students in math, language arts, life science, and art.

Lesson Plans: Responsible Pet Care

http://www.kindnews.org/teacher_zone/lesson_plans.asp
Lesson plans for grades preschool through sixth, covering language arts, social studies, math, science, and health.

Index